CHECKING
the Oil
AF350938
Marcy Schaaf
ADULT COLORING BOOK

WELCOME TO THE CAPTIVATING WORLD OF "CHECKING THE OIL," A UNIQUE ADULT COLORING BOOK CRAFTED BY THE TALENTED ARTIST MARCY SCHAAF. IN THIS COLLECTION, SCHAAF INVITES YOU TO IMMERSE YOURSELF IN A DELIGHTFUL FUSION OF CREATIVITY AND NOSTALGIA. THE TITLE, "CHECKING THE OIL," SERVES AS A PLAYFUL NOD TO A BYGONE ERA, BECKONING YOU TO EXPLORE THE CHARM OF VINTAGE AUTOMOBILES AND THE TIMELESS ALLURE OF THE OPEN ROAD.

MARCY SCHAAF'S INTRICATE ILLUSTRATIONS ARE MORE THAN JUST COLORING PAGES; THEY ARE WINDOWS INTO A WORLD WHERE CLASSIC CARS, WITH THEIR SLEEK CURVES AND TIMELESS DESIGNS, TAKE CENTER STAGE. EACH PAGE INVITES YOU TO UNLEASH YOUR IMAGINATION AND INFUSE VIBRANT HUES INTO THE BLACK-AND-WHITE CANVASES, BRINGING THESE AUTOMOTIVE MASTERPIECES TO LIFE.

AS YOU EMBARK ON THIS COLORING JOURNEY, YOU'LL DISCOVER A THERAPEUTIC ESCAPE FROM THE HUSTLE AND BUSTLE OF EVERYDAY LIFE. WHETHER YOU'RE AN AUTOMOTIVE ENTHUSIAST, AN ART AFICIONADO, OR SIMPLY SEEKING A MEDITATIVE PASTIME, "CHECKING THE OIL" PROMISES TO BE A DELIGHTFUL COMPANION. SO, GRAB YOUR FAVORITE COLORING TOOLS, LET YOUR CREATIVITY FLOW, AND ENJOY THE RELAXING AND REWARDING EXPERIENCE

PRAR

OIL

CHANG
RR OL OIL

CUTE

ANG.

GONTIAC

Find other adult coloring books at
www.BooksBySchaaf.com